THE CURE

of

DEPRESSION

and

EXCESSIVE SORROW

Richard Baxter

Bibliographic Information

Richard Baxter's sermon entitled, "The Cure of Melancholy and Overmuch Sorrow by Faith and Physick, Etc." was originally published in 1683. The text for this edition was taken from the 1838 edition of *The Practical Works of Richard Baxter*, Volume 4, published by GEORGE VIRTUE in London, England. The book title, spelling, language, and grammar have been gently updated.

Our goal is to provide high-quality, thought-provoking books that foster encouragement and spiritual growth. For more information regarding bulk purchases, other IP books, or our publishing services, visit us online or write to adam@ichthuspublications.com.

Copyright © 2015 Ichthus Publications
ISBN 13: 978-1517132880
ISBN 10: 1517132886

ICHTHUS
PUBLICATIONS

www.ichthuspublications.com

Printed in the United States of America

Contents

The Bible and Excessive Sorrow

Question. What are the best preservatives against depression and excessive sorrow?

"So you should rather turn to forgive and comfort him, or he may be overwhelmed by excessive sorrow" (2 Corinthians 2:7).

T HE BREVITY OF A sermon not allowing me time for any unnecessary work, I shall not stay to open the context, nor to inquire whether the person here spoken of be the same that is condemned for incest in 1 Corinthians 5* or some other; nor whether Chrysostom had good tradition for it, that it was a doctor of the church, or made such after his sin? Nor whether the late

---

* "It is actually reported that there is sexual immorality among you, and of a kind that is not tolerated even among pagans, for a man has his father's wife" (1 Cor. 5:1). See also verses 2-13.

expositor (Dr. Hammond) be in the right, who thence gathers that he was one of the bishops of Achaia; and that it was a synod of bishops that were to excommunicate him; who yet held that every congregation then had a bishop, and that he was to be excommunicated in the congregation; and that the people should not have followed or favoured such a teacher; it would have been no schism, or sinful separation, to have forsaken him? All that I now intend is, to open this last clause of the verse, which gives the reason why the censured sinner, being penitent, should be forgiven and comforted; lest he should be swallowed up with excessive sorrow; as it includeth these three doctrines, which I shall handle all together:

1. That sorrow, even for sin, may be excessive.

2. That excessive sorrow swalloweth one up.

3. Therefore it must be resisted and assuaged by necessary comfort, both by others, and by ourselves.

In handling these, I shall observe this order: (1.) I shall show you when sorrow is excessive. (2.) How excessive sorrow doth swallow a man up. (3.) What the causes of it are. (4.) What the cure is.

I. It is too notorious that excessive sorrow for sin is not the ordinary case of the world. A stupid, blockish disposition is the common cause of men's perdition. The plague of a hard heart, and seared conscience, keeps most from all due sense of sin, or danger, or misery, and of all the great and everlasting concerns of their guilty souls. A dead sleep in sin doth deprive most of the use of sense and understanding; they do some of the outward acts of religion as in a dream; they are vowed to God in baptism by others, and they profess to stand to it themselves; they go to church, and say over the words of the creed, and Lord's prayer, and commandments, they receive the Lord's Supper, and all as in a dream! They take on them to believe that sin is the most hateful thing to God, and hurtful to man, and yet they live in it with delight and obstinacy; they dream that they repent of it, when no persuasion will draw them to forsake it, and while they hate them that would cure them, and will not be as bad and mad as they who feel in them any effectual sorrow for what is past, or effectual sense of their present badness, or effectual resolution for a new and holy life. They dream that there is a judgment, a heaven, and a hell, but would they not be more affected with things of such unspeakable consequence if they were awake? Would they be wholly taken up with the matters of the flesh and world, and scarce have a serious thought or word of eternity, if they were awake?

Oh how sleepily and senselessly do they think, and talk, and bear of the great work of man's redemption by Christ, and of the need of justifying and sanctifying grace, and of the joys and miseries of the next life; and yet they say that they believe them! When we preach or talk to them of the greatest things, with the greatest evidence, and plainness, and earnestness that we can, we speak as to the dead, or to men asleep; they have ears, and hear not, nothing goeth to their hearts.

One would think that a man that reads in Scripture, and believes the everlasting glory offered, and the dreadful punishment threatened, and the necessity of holiness to salvation, and of a Saviour to deliver us from sin and hell, and how sure and near such a passage into the unseen world is to us all, should have much ado to moderate and bear the sense of such overwhelming things. But most men so little regard or feel them, that they have neither time nor heart to think of them as their concern, but hear of them as of some foreign land, where they have no interest, and which they never think to see. Yea, one would think by their senseless neglect of preparation, and their worldly minds and lives, that they were asleep, or in jest, when they confess that they must die; and that when they lay their friends in the grave, and see the skulls and bones cast up, they were but all this while in a dream, or did not believe that their turn is near.

Could we tell how to awaken sinners, they would come to themselves, and have other thoughts of these great things, and show it quickly by another kind of life.

all upon it, and take Christ for my Saviour and help: and then hope saith, I hope for this salvation by him: but melancholy, overwhelming sorrow and trouble is as great an adversary to this hope as water is to fire, or snow to heat. Despair is its very pulse and breath. Gladly such would have hope, but they cannot. All their thoughts are suspicious and misgiving, and they can see nothing but danger and misery, and a helpless state. And when hope, which is the anchor of the soul, is gone, what wonder if they be continually tossed with storms.

5. Excessive sorrow swalloweth up all comfortable sense of the infinite goodness and love of God, and thereby hindereth the soul from loving him; and in this it is an adversary to the very life of holiness. It is exceeding hard for such a troubled soul to apprehend the goodness of God at all, but much harder to judge that he is good and amiable to him: but as a man that in the deserts of Libya is scorched with the violent heats of the sun, and is ready to die with drought and faintness, may confess that the sun is the life of the earth and a blessing to mankind, but it is misery and death to him; even so, these souls, overwhelmed with grief, may say that God is good to others, but he seems an enemy to them, and to seek their destruction.

They think he hateth them, and hath forsaken them; and how can they love such a God who they think doth hate them, and resolve to damn them, and hath decreed them to it from eternity, and brought them into the world for no other end? They that can hardly love an enemy that doth but defame them, or oppress and wrong them, will more hardly love a God that they believe will damn them, and hath remedilessly appointed them thereto.

6. And then it must needs follow that this distemper is a false and injurious judge of all the word and works of God, and of all his mercies and corrections. Whatever such a one reads or hears, he thinks it all makes against him: every sad word and threatening in Scripture he thinks meaneth him, as if it named him. But the promises and comforts he hath no part in, as if he had been by name excepted.

All God's mercies are extenuated, and taken for no mercies, as if God intended them all but to make his sin the greater, and to increase his heavy reckoning and further Iris damnation. He thinks God doth but sugar over poison to him, and give him all in hatred, and not in any love, with a design to sink him the deeper in hell: and if God correct him, he supposeth that it is but the beginning of his misery, and God doth torment him before the time.

7. And by this you see that it is an enemy to thankfulness. It rather reproacheth God for his mercies,

as if they were injuries, than giveth him any hearty thanks.

8. And by this you may see that this distemper is quite contrary to the joy in the Holy Ghost, yea, and the peace in which God's kingdom much consisteth: nothing seemeth joyful unto such distressed souls. Delighting in God, and in his word and ways, is the flower and life of true religion. But these that I speak of can delight in nothing; neither in God, nor in his word, nor any duty. They do it as a sick man eateth his meat, for mere necessity, and with some loathing and averseness.

9. And all this showeth us that this disease is much contrary to the very prevailing course of the gospel. Christ came as a deliverer of the captives, a Saviour to reconcile us to God, and bring us glad tidings of pardon and everlasting joy: where the gospel was received it was great rejoicing, and so proclaimed by angels and by men. But all that Christ hath done, and purchased, and offered, and promised, seems nothing but matter of doubt and sadness to this disease.

10. Yea, it is a distemper which greatly advantageth Satan to cast in blasphemous thoughts of God, as if he were bad, and a hater and destroyer even of such as gladly would please him. The design of the devil is to describe God to us as like himself; who is a malicious enemy, and delighteth to do hurt: and if all men hate the devil for his

hurtfulness, would he not draw men to hate and blaspheme God, if he could make men believe that he is more hurtful?

The worshipping of God, as represented by an image is odious to him, because it seems to make him like such a creature as that image representeth. How much more blasphemous is it to feign him to be like the malicious devils! Diminutive, low thoughts of his goodness, as well as of his greatness, is a sin which greatly injureth God: as if you should think that he is no better or trustier than a father or a friend, much more to think him such as distempered souls imagine him. You would wrong his ministers if you should describe them as Christ doth the false prophets, as hurtful thorns, and thistles, and wolves. And is it not worse to think far worse than this of God?

11. This excessive sorrow doth unfit men for all profitable meditation; it confounds their thoughts, and turneth them to hurtful distractions and temptations; and the more they muse, the more they are overwhelmed. And it turneth prayer into mere complaint, instead of child-like believing supplications. It quite undisposeth the soul to God's feeding, and especially to a comfortable sacramental communion, and fetcheth greater terror from it, lest unworthy receiving will but hasten and increase their damnation. And it rendereth preaching and counsel too oft unprofitable: say what you will that is

never so convincing, either it doth not change them, or is presently lost.

12. And it is a distemper which maketh all sufferings more heavy, as facing upon a poor diseased soul, and having no comfort to set against it: and it maketh death exceeding terrible, because they think it will be the gate of hell; so that life seemeth burdensome to them, and death terrible; they are weary of living, and afraid of dying. Thus excessive sorrow swalloweth up.

4

The Causes and Cure of Depression

Question. What are the causes and cure of it?

WITH VERY MANY THERE is a great part of the cause in distemper, weakness, and diseasedness of the body, and by it the soul is greatly disabled to any comfortable sense. But the more it ariseth from such natural necessity, it is the less sinful, and less dangerous to the soul, but never the less troublesome, but the more.

Three diseases cause excessive sorrow.

1. Those that consist in such violent pain as natural strength is unable to bear; but this being usually not very long, is not now to be chiefly spoken of.

2. A natural passionateness, and weakness of that reason that should quiet passion. It is too frequent a case with aged persons that are much debilitated, to be very apt to offense and; and children cannot choose but cry

when they are hurt; but it is most troublesome and hurtful to many women, (and some men), who are so easily troubled, and hardly quieted, that they have very little power on themselves; even many who fear God, and who have very sound understandings, and quick wits, have almost no more power against troubling passions, anger, and grief, but especially fear, than they have of any other persons.

Their very natural temper is a strong disease of troubling, sorrow, fear, and displeasedness. They that are not melancholy, are yet of so childish, and sick, and impatient a temper, that one thing or other is still either discontenting, grieving, or affrighting them. They are like an aspen leaf, still shaking with the least motion of the air. The wisest and most patient man cannot please and justify such a one; a word, yea, or a look, offendeth them; every sad story, or news, or noise, affrighteth them; and as children must have all that they cry for before they will be quiet, so is it with too many such. The case is very sad to those about them, but much more to themselves. To dwell with the sick in the house of mourning is less uncomfortable. But yet while reason is not overthrown, the case is not remediless, nor wholly excusable.

3. But when the brain and imagination are impaired, and reason partly overthrown by the disease called melancholy, this maketh the cure yet more difficult; for

commonly it is the foresaid persons, whose natural temper is timorous and passionate, and apt to discontent and grief, who fall into infirmity and melancholy; and the conjunction of both the natural temper and the disease does increase the misery.

The signs of such diseasing melancholy I have often elsewhere described. As,

I. The trouble and disquiet of the mind doth then become a settled habit; they can see nothing but matter of fear and trouble. All that they hear or do doth feed it; danger is still before their eyes; all that they read and hear makes against them; they can delight in nothing; fearful dreams trouble them when they sleep, and distracted thoughts do keep them long waking; it offends them to see another laugh, or be merry; they think that every beggars case is happier than theirs; they will hardly believe that anyone else is in their case, when some two or three in a week, or a day, come to me in the same case, so like, that you would think it were the same person's case which they all express; they have no pleasure in relations, friends, estate, or anything; they think that God hath forsaken them, and that the day of grace is past, and there is no more hope; they say they cannot pray, but howl, and groan, and God will not hear them; they will not believe that they have any sincerity and grace; they say they cannot repent, they cannot believe, but that their hearts are utterly hardened; usually they are afraid lest they have committed the unpardonable sin against the Holy Ghost: in a word, fears, and troubles, and almost despair, are the constant temper of their minds.

2. If you convince them that they have some evidences of sincerity, and that their fears are causeless, and injurious to themselves, and unto God, and they have nothing to say against it, yet either it takes off none of their trouble, or else it returneth the next day; for the cause remaineth in their bodily disease; quiet them a hundred times, and their fears a hundred times return.

3. Their misery is, that what they think they cannot choose but think. You may almost as well persuade a man not to shake in a fever, or not to feel when he is pained, as persuade them to cast away their self-troubling thoughts, or not to think all the enormous, confounding thoughts as they do, they cannot get them out of their heads night or day. Tell them that they must forbear long musings, which disturb them, and they cannot. Tell them that they must cast out false imaginations out of their minds, when Satan casts them in, and must turn their thoughts to something else, and they cannot do it. Their thoughts and troubles, and fears, are gone out of their power, and the more, by how much the more melancholy and impaired they are.

4. And when they are grown to this, usually they seem to feel something besides themselves, as it were, speak in them, and saying this and that to them, and bidding them to do this or that; and they will tell you now it saith this or that, and tell you when and what it hath said to them, and they will hardly believe how much of it is the disease of their own imagination.

5. In this case they are exceeding prone to think they have revelations; and whatever comes into their minds they think some revelation brought it thither. They use to say, this text of Scripture at such a time was set upon my mind, and that text at another time was set on my mind; when oft the sense that they took them in was false, or a false application of it made to themselves, and perhaps several texts applied to contrary conclusions, as if one gave them hope, and another contradicted it.

And some of them hereupon are very prone to prophecies, and verily believe that God hath foretold them this or that, till they see that it cometh not to pass, and then they are ashamed.

And many of them turn heretics, and take up errors in religion, believing verily that God believed them, and set such things upon their minds: and some of them that were long troubled, get quietness and joy by such changes of their opinions, thinking that now they are in God's way, which they were out of all this while, and therefore it was that they had no comfort. Of these I have known divers persons comforted that have fallen into the clean contrary opinions; some have turned papists and superstitious, and some have run too far from papists, and some have had comfort by turning Anabaptists, some antinomians, some contrarily called Arminians, some perfectionists, some Quakers; and some have turned from Christianity itself to infidelity, and denied the life to come, and have lived in licentious uncleanness. But these melancholy heretics and apostates usually by this cast off their sadness, and are not the sort that I have now to deal with.

6. But the sadder, better sort, feeling this talk and stir within them, are oft apt to be confident that they are possessed by the devil, or at least bewitched, of which I will say more anon.

7. And most of them are violently haunted with blasphemous suggestions of ideas, at which they tremble, and yet cannot keep them out of their mind; either they are tempted and haunted to doubt of the Scripture, or Christianity, or the life to come, or to think some ill of God; and oftentimes they are strangely urged, as by something in them, to speak some blasphemous word of God, or to renounce him, and they tremble at the suggestion, and yet it still followeth them, and some poor souls yield to it, and say some bad word against God, and

then, as soon as it is spoken, somewhat within them saith, Now thy damnation is sealed, thou hast sinned against the Holy Ghost, there is no hope.

8. When it is far gone, they are tempted to lay some law upon themselves never to speak more, or not to eat, and some of them have famished themselves to death.

9. And when it is far gone, they often think that they have apparitions, and this and that likeness appeareth to them, especially lights in the night about their beds. And sometimes they are confident that they hear voices, and feel something touch or hurt them.

10. They fly from company, and can do nothing but sit alone and muse.

11. They cast off all business, and will not be brought to any diligent labour in their callings.

12. And when it cometh to extremity, they are weary of their lives, and strongly followed with temptations to make away themselves, as if something within them were urging them either to drown themselves, or cut their own throats, or hang themselves, or cast themselves headlong, which, alas! Too many have done.

13. And if they escape this, when it is ripe, they become quite distracted.

These are the doleful symptoms and effects of melancholy; and therefore how desirable is it to prevent them, or to be cured while it is but beginning, before they fall into so sad a state!

And here it is necessary that I answer the doubt whether such persons be possessed with the devil, or not? And how much of all this aforesaid is from him?

And I must tell the melancholy person that is sincere, that the knowledge of the devil's agency in his case, may be more to his comfort than to his despair.

And first, we must know what is meant by Satan's possession, either of the body or the soul? It is not merely his local presence and abode in a man that is called his possession, for we know little of that, how far he is more present with a bad man than a good, but it is his exercising power on a man by such a stated, effectual operation. As the Spirit of God is present with the worst, and maketh many holy motions to the souls of the impenitent, but he is a settled powerful agent in the soul of a believer, and so is said to dwell in such, and to possess them, by the habit of holiness and love; even so Satan maketh too frequent motions to the faithful, but he possesseth only the souls of the ungodly by predominant habits of unbelief and sensuality.

And so also he is permitted by God to inflict persecutions, and crosses, and ordinary diseases, on the just; but when he is God's executioner of extraordinary plagues, especially on the head, depriving men of sense and understanding, and working above the bare nature of the disease, this is called his possession.

And as most evil notions on the soul have Satan for their father, and our own hearts as the mothers, so most or many bodily diseases are by Satan, permitted by God, though there be causes of them also in the body itself. And when our own miscarriages, and humours, and the season, weather, and accidents, may be causes, yet Satan may, by these, be a superior cause.

And when his operations are such as we call a possession, yet he may work by means and bodily dispositions, and sometimes he worketh quite above the power of the disease itself, as when the unlearned speak in strange languages, and when bewitched persons vomit iron, glass, etc. And sometimes he doth only work by the disease itself as in epilepsies, madness, etc.

5

Demonic Causes of Depression

F ROM ALL THIS IT IS easy to gather, 1. That for Satan to possess the body is no certain sign of a graceless state, nor will this condemn the soul of any, if the soul itself be not possessed. Nay, there are few of God's children but it is like are sometimes afflicted by Satan, as the executioner of God's correcting them, and sometimes of God's trials, as in the case of Job; whatsoever some say to the contrary, it is likely that the prick in the flesh, which was Satan's messenger to buffet Paul, was some such pain as the stone, which yet was not removed, that we find, after thrice praying, but only he had a promise of sufficient grace.

2. Satan's possession of an ungodly soul is the miserable case, which is a thousand times worse than his possessing of the body; but every corruption or sin is not such a possession, for no man is perfect without sin.

3. No sin proveth Satan's damnable possession of a man but that which he loveth more than he hateth it, and which he had rather keep than leave, and willfully keepeth.

4. And this is matter of great comfort to such melancholy, honest souls, if they have but understanding to receive it, that of all men none love their sin which they groan under so little as they; yea, it is the heavy burden of their souls. Do you love your unbelief, your fears, your distracted thoughts, your temptations to blasphemy? Had you rather keep them than be delivered from them? The proud man, the ambitious, the fornicator, the drunkard, the gamester, the time-wasting gallants that sit out hours at cards, and plays, and idle chats, the gluttonous pleasers of the appetite, all these love their sins, and would not leave them; as Esau sold his birth right for one morsel, they will venture the loss of God, of Christ, and soul, and heaven, rather than leave a swinish sin. But is this your case? Do you so love your sad condition? You are weary of it, and heavy laden, and therefore are called to come to Christ for ease (Matt. 11:28-29).

5. And it is the devil's way, if he can, to haunt those with troubling temptations whom he cannot overcome with alluring and damning temptations. As he raiseth storms of persecution against them without, as soon as

they are escaping from his deceits, so doth he trouble them within, as far as God permitteth him.

We deny not but Satan hath a great hand in the case of such melancholy persons; for,

1. His temptations caused the sin which God corrects them for.

2. His execution usually is a cause of the distemper of the body.

3. And, as a tempter, he is the cause of the sinful and troublesome thoughts, and doubts, and fears, and passions, which the melancholy causeth. The devil cannot do what he will with us, but what we give him advantage to do. He cannot break open our doors, but he can enter if we leave them open. He can easily tempt a heavy, phlegmatic body to sloth, a weak and choleric person to anger, a strong and sanguine man to lust, and one of a strong appetite to gluttony or to drunkenness, and vain, sportful youth to idle plays, and gaming, and voluptuousness, when to others such temptations would have small strength.

And so, if he can cast you into despair, he can easily tempt you to excessive sorrow and fear, and to distracting doubts and thoughts, and to murmur against God, and to despair, and still think that you are undone, undone; and even to blasphemous thoughts of God; or, if it take not this way, then to fanatic conceits of revelation, and a prophesying spirit.

6. But I add, that God will not impute his mere temptations to you, but to himself, be they never so bad, as long as you receive them not by the will, but hate them; nor will he condemn you for those ill effects which are unavoidable from the power of a bodily disease, any more than he will condemn a man for raving thoughts, or words in a fever, frenzy, or utter madness. But so far as reason yet hath power, and the will can govern passions, it is your fault if you use not the power, though the difficulty make the fault the less.

6

More Usual Causes of Depression

B UT USUALLY OTHER causes go before this disease of
melancholy, (except in some bodies naturally prone
to it), and therefore, before I speak of the cure of it, I will
briefly touch them.

And one of the most common causes is sinful
impatience, discontents, and cares, proceeding from a
sinful love of some bodily interest, and from a lack of
sufficient submission to the will of God, and trust in him,
and taking heaven for a satisfying portion.

I must necessarily use all these words to show the
true nature of this complicated disease of souls. The
names tell you that it is a conjunction of many sins, which
in themselves are of no small malignity, and were they the
predominant bent and habit of heart and life, they would
be the signs of a graceless state; but while they are hated,
and overcome not grace, but our heavenly portion is more

esteemed, and chosen, and sought than earthly prosperity, the mercy of God, through Christ, doth pardon it, and will at last deliver us from all. But yet it beseemeth even a pardoned sinner to know the greatness of his sin, that he may not favour it, nor be unthankful for forgiveness.

I will therefore distinctly open the parts of this sin which bringeth many into dismal melancholy.

It is presupposed that God trieth his servants in this life with manifold afflictions, and Christ will have us bear the cross, and follow him in submissive patience. Some are tried with painful diseases, and some with wrong by enemies, and some with the unkindness of friends, and some with froward, provoking relatives and company, and some with slanders, and some with persecution, and many with losses, disappointments, and poverty.

1. And here impatience is the beginning of the working of the sinful malady. Our natures are all too regardful of the interest of the flesh, and too weak in bearing heavy burdens; and poverty hath those trials which full and wealthy persons, that feel them not, too little pity, especially in two cases.

1. When men have not themselves only, but wives and children in want, to quiet. When they are in debt to others, which is a heavy burden to a candid mind, though thievish borrowers make too light of it. In these straits

and trials, men are apt to be too sensible and impatient. When they and their families need food, and raiment, and fire, and other necessaries to the body, and know not which way to get supply; when landlords, and butchers, and bakers, and other creditors, are calling for their debts, and they have it not to pay them; it is hard to keep all this from going too near the heart, and hard to bear it with obedient, quiet submission to God, especially for women, whose nature is weak, and liable to too much passion.

2. And this impatience turneth to a settled discontent and unquietness of spirit, which affecteth the body itself, and lieth all day as a load, or continual trouble at the heart.

3. And impatience and discontent do set the thoughts on the rack with grief and continual cares how to be eased of the troubling cause; they can scarce think of anything else, and these cares do even feed upon the heart, and are, to the mind, as a consuming fever to the body.

4. And the secret root or cause of all this is the worst part of the sin, which is, too much love to the body, and this world. Were nothing over-loved, it would have no power to torment us. If ease and health were not over-loved, pain and sickness would be the more tolerable; if children and friends were not over-loved, the death of them would not overwhelm us with inordinate sorrow; if

the body were not over-loved, and worldly wealth and prosperity overvalued, it were easy to endure hard fare, and labour, and lack, not only of superfluities and conveniences, but even of that which is necessary to health, yea, or life itself, if God will have it so, at least, to avoid vexations, discontents, and cares, and inordinate grief and trouble of mind.

5. There is yet more sin in the root of all, and that is, it showeth that our wills are yet too selfish, and not subdued to a due submission to the will of God, but we would be as gods to ourselves, and be at our own choosing, and must needs have what the flesh desireth. We need a due resignation of ourselves and all our concerns to God, and live not as children, in due dependence on him for our daily bread, but must needs be the keepers of our own provision.

6. And this showeth that we be not sufficiently humbled for our sin, or else we should be thankful for the lowest state, as being much better than that which we deserved.

7. And there is apparently much distrust of God and unbelief in these troubling discontents and cares. Could we trust God as well as ourselves, or as we could trust a faithful friend, or as a child can trust his father, how quiet would our minds be in the sense of his wisdom, all-sufficiency, and love!

8. And this unbelief yet hath a worse effect than worldly trouble: it showeth that men take not the love of God and the heavenly glory for their sufficient portion; unless they may have what they lack, or would have, for the body in this world, unless they may be free from poverty, and crosses, and provocations, and injuries, and pains, all that God hath promised them here or hereafter, even everlasting glory, will not satisfy them; and when God, and Christ, and heaven, are not enough to quiet a man's mind, he is in great need of faith, hope, and love, which are far greater matters than food and raiment.

III. Another great cause of such trouble of mind is the guilt of some great and willful sin; when conscience is convinced, and yet the soul is not converted; sin is beloved, and yet feared; God's wrath doth terrify them, and yet not enough to overcome their sin. Some live in secret fraud and robbery, and many in drunkenness, in secret fleshly lusts, either self-pollution or fornication, and they know that for such things the wrath of God cometh on the children of disobedience; and yet the rage of appetite and lust prevaileth, and they despair and sin; and while the sparks of hell fall on their consciences, it changeth neither heart nor life: there is some more hope of the recovery of these than of dead-hearted or unbelieving sinners, who work uncleanness with greediness, as being past feeling, and blinded to defend their sins, and plead against holy obedience to God. Brutishness is not so bad as diabolism and malignity. But none of these are the persons spoken of in my text; their sorrow is not excessive, but too little, as long as it will not restrain them from their sin.

But yet, if God convert these persons, the sins which they now live in may possibly hereafter plunge their souls into such depths of sorrow in the review as may swallow them up.

And when men truly converted yet dally with the bait, and renew the wounds of their consciences by their lapses, it is no wonder if their sorrow and terrors are renewed. Grievous sins have fastened so on the conscience of many, as have cast them into incurable melancholy and distraction.

7

Depression and Sin for Christians

B UT, AMONG PEOPLE fearing God, there is yet another cause of melancholy, and of sorrowing excessive, and that is, ignorance and mistakes in matters which their peace and comfort are concerned in. I will name some particulars.

1. One is, ignorance of the prevailing course of the gospel or covenant of grace, as some libertines, called antinomians, more dangerously mistake it, who tell men that Christ hath repented and believed them, and that they must no more question their faith and repentance, than they must question the righteousness of Christ: so many better Christians understand not that the gospel is tidings of unspeakable joy to all that will believe it; and that Christ and life are offered freely to them that will accept him, and that no sins, however great or many soever, are excepted from pardon, to the soul that

unfeignedly turneth to God by faith in Christ; and that whoever will may freely take the water of life, and all that are weary and athirst are invited to come to him for ease and rest.

And they seem not to understand the conditions of forgiveness, which is but true consent to the pardoning, saving covenant.

2. And many of them are mistaken about the use of sorrow for sin, and about the nature of hardness of heart: they think that if their sorrow be not so passionate as to bring forth tears, and greatly to afflict them, they are not capable of pardon, though they should consent to all the pardoning covenant; and they consider not that it is not our sorrow for itself that God delighteth in but it is the taking down of pride, and that so much humbling sense of sin, danger, and misery, as may make us feel the need of Christ and mercy, and bring us unfeignedly to consent to be his disciples, and to be saved upon his covenant terms. Be sorrow much or little, if it do this much the sinner shall be saved.

And as to the length of God's sorrow, some think that the pangs of the new birth must be a long-continued state; whereas we read in the Scripture, that, by the penitent sinners the gospel was still received speedily with joy, as being the gift of Christ, and pardon, and everlasting life: humility and loathing must continue and increase, but our first great sorrows may be swallowed up with holy thankfulness and joy.

And as for hardness of heart, in Scripture, it is taken for such a stiff, rebellious obstinacy, as will not be moved from their sins to obedience by any of God's commands or threats, and is called oft an iron sinew, a stiff neck, etc.; but it is never taken for the mere absence of tears or passionate sorrow in a man that is willing to obey: the hard-hearted are the rebellious. Sorrow, even for sin, may be excessive, and a passionate woman or man may easily grieve and weep for the sin which they will not leave; but obedience cannot be too much.

3. And very many are cast down by ignorance of themselves, not knowing the sincerity which God hath given them. Grace is weak in the best of us here, and little and weak grace is not very easily perceived, for it acteth weakly and unconstantly, and it is known but by its acts; and weak grace is always joined with too strong corruption; and all sin in heart and life is contrary to grace, and doth obscure it; and such persons usually have too little knowledge, and are too strange at home, and unskillful in examining and watching their heart and keeping its accounts: and how can any, under all these hindrances, yet keep any full assurance of their own sincerity.

If, with much ado, they get some assurances, neglect of duty, or coldness in it, or yielding to temptation, or unconstancy in close obedience, will make them question all again, and ready to say it was all but hypocrisy. And a sad and melancholy frame of mind is always apt to conclude the worst, and hardly brought to see anything that is good, and tends to comfort.

4. And in such a case there are too few that know how to fetch comfort from bare probabilities, when they get not certainty, much less from the mere offers of grace and salvation, even when they cannot deny but they are willing to accept them; and if none should have comfort but those that have assurance of their sincerity and salvation, despair would swallow up the souls of most, even of true believers.

5. And ignorance of other men increaseth the fears and sorrows of some. They think, by our preaching and writing, that we are much better than we are; and then they think that they are graceless, because they come short of our supposed measures; whereas if they dwelt with us, and saw our failings, or knew us as well as we know ourselves, or saw all our sinful thoughts and vicious dispositions written in our foreheads, they would be cured of this error.

6. And unskillful teachers do cause the griefs and perplexities of very many. Some cannot open to them

clearly the prevailing course of the covenant of grace: some are themselves unacquainted with any spiritual, heavenly consolations; and many have no experience of any inward holiness, and renewal by the Holy Ghost, and know not what sincerity is, nor wherein a saint doth differ from an ungodly sinner, as wicked deceivers make good and bad to differ but a little, if not the best to be taken for the worst; so some unskillful men do place sincerity in such things as are not so much as duty, as the papists in their manifold inventions and superstitions, and many sects in their unsound opinions.

And some unskillfully and unsoundly describe the state of grace, and tell you how far a hypocrite may go, so as unjustly discourageth and confoundeth the weaker sort of Christians, and cannot amend the mis-expression of their books or teachers; and too many teachers laymen's comforts, if not salvation, on controversies which are past their reach, and pronounce heresy and damnation against that which they themselves understand not. Even the Christian world, these one thousand three hundred, or one thousand two hundred years, is divided into parties by the teachers' unskillful quarrels about words which they took in several senses. Is it any wonder if the hearers of such are distracted?

IV. I have told you the causes of distracted sorrows, I am now to tell you what is the cure; but, alas! It is not so soon done as told; and I shall begin where the disease beginneth, and tell you both what the patient himself must do, and what must be done by his friends and teachers.

I. Look not on the sinful part of your troubles, either as better or worse than indeed it is.

1. Too many persons in their sufferings and sorrows think they are only to be pitied, and take little notice of the sin that caused them, or that they still continue to commit; and too many unskillful friends and ministers do only comfort them, when a round chiding and discovery of their sin should be the better part of the cure; and if they were more sensible how much sin there is, in their overvaluing the world, and not trusting God, and in their hard thoughts of him, and their poor, unholy thoughts of his goodness, and in their undervaluing the heavenly glory, which should satisfy them in the most afflicted state, and in their daily impatiences, cares, and discontents, and in denying the mercies or graces received, this would do more to cure some than words of comfort, when they say as Jonah, "I do well to be angry," and think that all their denials of grace, and distracting sorrows and wrangling against God's love and mercy, are their duties, it is time to make them know how great sinners they are.

2. And yet when as foolishly they think that all these sins are marks of a graceless state, and that God will take the devil's temptations for sins, and condemn them for that which they abhor, and take their very disease of melancholy for a crime, this also needs confutation and reprehension, that they may not by error cherish their passions or distress.

II. Particularly, give not way to a habit of peevish impatience: though it is carnal love to somewhat more than to God and glory which is the damning sin, yet impatience must not pass for innocence. Did you not reckon upon sufferings, and of bearing the cross, when you first gave up yourselves to Christ? And do you think it strange? Look for it, and make it your daily study to prepare for any trial that God may bring you to, and then it will not surprise you, and overwhelm you. Prepare for the loss of children and friends, for the loss of goods, and for poverty and want; prepare for slanders, injuries, or poisons, for sickness, pain, and death. It is your unpreparedness that maketh it seem unsufferable.

And remember that it is but a vile body that suffereth, which you always knew must suffer death, and rot to dust: and whoever is the instrument of your sufferings, it is God that trieth you by it; and when you think that you are only displeased with men, you are not guiltless of murmuring against God, or else his overruling hand would persuade you to submissive patience.

Especially make conscience of a settled discontent of mind. Have you not yet much better than you deserve? And do you forget how many years you have enjoyed undeserving mercy? Discontent is a continued resistance of God's disposing will, that I say not some rebellion against it. Your own wills rise up against the will of God. It is atheistical to think that your sufferings are not by his providence; and dare you repine against God, and continue in such repining? To whom else doth it belong to dispose of you and all the world?

And when you feel distracting cares for your deliverances, remember that this is not trusting God. Care for your own duty, and obey his command, but leave it to him what you shall have; tormenting cares do but add to your afflictions; it is a great mercy of God that he forbiddeth you these cares, and promiseth to care for you. Your Saviour himself hath largely, though gently, reprehended them (Matt. 6), and told you how sinful and unprofitable they are, and that your Father knoweth what you need; and if he deny it you, it is for just cause, and if it be to correct you, it is yet to profit you; and if you submit to him, and accept his gift, he will give you much better than he taketh from you, even Christ and everlasting life.

III. Set yourselves more diligently than ever to overcome the inordinate love of the world. It will be a happy use of all your troubles if you can follow them up to the fountain, and find out what it is that you cannot bear the absence or loss of, and consequently what is it that you over-love. God is very jealous, even when he loveth, against every idol that is loved too much, and with any of that love which is due to him. And if he take them all away, and tear them out of our hands and hearts, it is merciful as well as just.

I speak not this to those that are troubled only for need of more faith, and holiness, and communion with God, and assurance of salvation. These troubles might give them much comfort if they understood aright from whence they come, and what they signify. For as impatient trouble under worldly crosses doth prove that a man loveth the world too much, so impatient trouble, for need of more holiness and communion with God, doth show that such are lovers of holiness and of God. Love goeth before desire and grief. That which men love they delight in if they have it, and mourn for absence of it, and desire to obtain it. The will is the love; and no man is troubled for lack of that which he would not have.

But the commonest cause of passionate melancholy is at first some worldly discontent and care; either hardships or crosses, or the fear of suffering, or the unsuitableness and provocation of some related to them, or disgrace, or contempt, do cast them into passionate discontent, and self-will cannot bear the denial of something which they would have, and then when the discontent hath muddied and diseased a man's mind, temptations about his soul do come in afterwards; and that which begun only with worldly crosses, doth after seem to be all about religion, conscience, or merely for sin and lack of grace.

Why could you not patiently bear the words, the wrongs, the losses, the crosses, that did befall you? Why made you so great a matter of these bodily, transitory things? Is it not because you over-loved them? Were you not in good earnest when you called them vanity, and covenanted to leave them to the will of God? Would you have God let you alone in so great a sin as the love of the world, or giving any of his due to creatures?

If God should not teach you what to love, and what to set light by, and cure you of so dangerous a disease as a fleshly, earthly mind, he should not sanctify you, and fit you for heaven. Souls go not to heaven as an arrow is shot upward, against their inclination; but as fire naturally tendeth upward, and earth downward, to their like; so when holy men are dead, their souls have a natural inclination upward; and it is their love that is their inclination; they love God, and heaven, and holy company, and their old godly friends, and holy works, even mutual love, and the joyful praises of Jehovah. And this spirit and love is as a fiery nature, which carrieth them heavenward; and angels convey them not thither by force, but conduct them as a bride to her marriage, who is carried all the way by love.

And on the other side, the souls of wicked men are of a fleshly, worldly inclination, and love not heavenly works and company, and have nothing in them to carry them to God; but they love worldly trash, and sensual, bestial delights, though they cannot enjoy them; and as poor men love riches, and are vexed for the absence of what they love; and therefore it is no wonder if wicked souls do dwell with devils in the lower regions, and that they make apparitions here when God permits them, and if holy souls be liable to no such descent. Love is the soul's poise and spring, and carrieth souls downward or upward accordingly.

Away, then, with the earthly, fleshly love. How long will you stay here; and what will earth and flesh do for you? So far as it may be helpful to holiness and heaven, God will not deny it to submissive children; but to over-love is to turn from God, and is the dangerous malady of souls, and the poise that sinks them down from heaven. Had you learned better to forsake all for Christ, and to account all but as loss and dung, as Paul did (Phil. 3:8), you could more easily bear the lack of it. When did you see any live in discontent, and distracted with melancholy, grief, and cares, for lack of dung, or a bubble, a shadow, or a merry dream? If you will not otherwise know the world, God will otherwise make you know it to your sorrow.

IV. If you are not satisfied that God alone, Christ alone, heaven alone, is enough for you, as matter of felicity and full content, go, study the case better, and you may be convinced. Go, learn better your catechism, and the principles of religion, and then you will learn to lay up a treasure in heaven, and not on earth, and to know that it is best to be with Christ; and that death, which blasteth all the glory of the world, and equalleth rich and poor, is the common door to heaven or hell: and then conscience will not ask you whether you have lived in pleasure or in pain, in riches or in poverty; but whether you have lived to God or to the flesh; for heaven or for earth? And what hath had the pre-eminence in your hearts and lives?

If there be shame in heaven, you will be ashamed when you are there, that you whined and murmured for the lack of any thing that the flesh desired upon earth, and went thither grieving because our bodies suffered here. Study more to live by faith and hope, on the unseen promised glory with Christ, and you will patiently endure any sufferings in the way.

˙ V. And study better how great a sin it is to set our own wills and desires in a discontented opposition to the wisdom, will, and providence of God; and to make our wills instead of his, as gods to ourselves. Does not a murmuring heart secretly accuse God? All accusation of God hath some degree of blasphemy in it. For the accuser supposeth that somewhat of God is to be blamed, and if you dare not open your mouths to accuse him, let not the repinings of your hearts accuse him; know how much of religion and holiness consisteth in bringing this rebellious self-will to a full resignation, submission, and conformity to the will of God. Till you can rest in God's will you will never have rest.

VI. And study well how great a duty it is wholly to trust God, and our blessed Redeemer, both with soul and body, and all we have. Is not infinite power, wisdom, and goodness, to be trusted? Is not a Savior, who came from heaven into flesh, to save sinners by such incomprehensible ways of love, to be trusted with that which he hath so dearly bought? To whom else will you trust? Is it yourselves, or your friends? Who is it that hath kept you all your lives, and done all for you that is done? Who is it that hath saved all the souls that are now in heaven? What is our Christianity but a life of faith? And is this your faith, to distract yourselves with care and troubles, if God do not fit all his providences to your wills?

Seek first his kingdom and righteousness, and he hath promised that all other thin shall be added to you, and not a hair of your head shall perish, for they are all, as it were, numbered. A sparrow falls not to the ground without his providence, and doth he set less by those that fain would please him? Believe God, and trust him, and your cares, and fears, and griefs will vanish.

Oh, that you knew what a mercy and comfort it is for God to make it your duty to trust him! If he had made you no promise, this is equal to a promise. If he does but bid you trust him, you may be sure he will not deceive your trust. If a faithful friend that is able to relieve you, do but bid you trust him for your relief, you will not think that he will deceive you.

Alas! I have friends that durst trust *me* with their estates, and lives, and souls, if they were in my power, and would not fear that I would destroy or hurt them, that yet cannot trust the *God* of infinite goodness with them, though he both commands them to trust him, and promise them he will never fail them nor forsake them. It is the refuge of my soul, that quieteth me in my fears, that God, my Father and Redeemer, hath commanded me to trust him with my body, my health, my liberty, my estate, and when eternity seemeth strange and dreadful to me, that he bids me trust him with my departing soul! Heaven and earth are upheld and maintained by him, and shall I distrust him?

Objection. But it is none but his children that he will save.

Answer. True; and all are his children that are truly willing to obey and please him. If you are truly willing to be holy, and to obey his commanding will, in a godly, righteous, and sober life, you may boldly rest in his disposing will, and rejoice in his rewarding and accepting will, for he will pardon all our infirmities through the merits and intercession of Christ.

VII. If you would not be swallowed up with sorrow, swallow not the baits of sinful pleasure. Passions, and dullness, and defective duties have their degrees of guilt, but it is pleasing sin that is the dangerous and deep-wounding sin. Oh, fly from the baits of lust, and pride, and ambition, and covetousness, and an unruly appetite to drink or meat, as you would fly from guilt, and grief, and terror. The more pleasure you have in sin, usually the more sorrow it will bring you; and the more you know it to be sin, and conscience tells you that God is against it, and yet you will go on, and bear down conscience, the sharper will conscience afterwards afflict you, and the less will it be quieted when it is awakened to repentance.

Yea, when a humbled soul is pardoned by grace, and believeth that he is pardoned, he will not easily forgive himself. The remembrance of the willfulness of sinning, and how base a temptation prevailed with us, and what mercies and motives we bore down, will make us so displeased and angry with ourselves, and so to loathe such naughty hearts, as will not admit a speedy or easy reconciliation.

Indeed, when we remember that we sinned against knowledge, even when we remembered that God did see us, and that we offended him, it will keep up long doubts of our sincerity in the soul, and make us afraid lest still we have the same hearts, and should again do the same if we had the same temptations. Never look for joy or peace as long as you live in willful and beloved sin. This thorn must be taken out of your hearts before you will be eased of the pain, unless God leave you to a senseless heart, and Satan give you a deceitful peace, which doth but prepare for greater sorrow.

VIII. But if none of the aforementioned sins cause your sorrows, but they come from the mere perplexities of your mind about religion, or the state of your souls, as fearing God's wrath for your former sins, or doubting of your sincerity and salvation, then these foregoing reproofs are not meant to such as you; but I shall now lay you down your proper remedy, and that is, the cure of that ignorance and those errors which cause your troubles.

1. Many are perplexed about controversies in religion, while every contending party is confident, and hath a great deal to say, which to the ignorant seemeth like to truth, and which the hearer cannot answer, and when each party tells them that their way is the only way, and threateneth damnation to them if they turn not to them. The papists say, "There is no salvation out of our church; that is, to none but the subjects of the bishop of Rome." The Greeks condemn them, and extol their church, and every party extols their own. Yea, some will convert them with fire and sword, and say, "Be of our church, or lie in gaol; or make their church itself a prison, by driving in the incapable and unwilling."

Question. Among all these, how shall the ignorant know what to choose?

Answer. The case is sad, and yet not so sad as the case of the far greatest part of the world, who are quiet in heathenism, or infidelity, or never trouble themselves about religion, but follow the customs of their countries, and the prince's laws, that they may not suffer. It is some sign of a regard to God and your salvation, that you are troubled about religion, and careful to know which is the right; even controversy is better than atheistical indifference, that will be on the upper side, be it what will.

If you cast acorns or pulse among them, swine will strive for it; or if it be carrion, dogs will fight for it; but if it be gold or jewels, dogs and swine will never strive for them, but tread them in the dirt. But cast them before men, and they will be all together by the ears for them. Lawyers contend about law, and princes about dominion, which others mind not; and religious persons strive about religions; and what wonder is this? It doth but show that they value their souls and religion, and that their understandings are yet imperfect. But if you will follow these plain directions, controversies need not break your peace.

8

Ten Rules for Settling the Heart

SEE THAT YOU BE TRUE to the light and law of nature, which all mankind is obliged to observe. If you had no Scripture nor Christianity, nature (that is, the works of God) do tell you that there is a God, and that he is the rewarder of them that diligently seek him. It tells you that God is absolutely perfect in power, knowledge, and goodness, and that man is a reasonable, free agent made by him, and therefore is his own, and at his will and government. It tells you that a man's actions are not indifferent, but some things we ought to do, and some things we ought not to do; and that virtue and vice, moral good and evil, do greatly differ; and therefore that there is some universal law which obligeth us to the good, and forbids the evil, and that this can be none but the law of the universal Governor, which is God. It tells all men that they owe this God their absolute obedience, because he is their most wise and absolute Ruler; and that they owe him their chiefest love, because he is not only the chief Benefactor, but also most perfectly amiable in himself. It tells us that he hath made us all sociable members of one world, and that we owe love and help to one another. It tells us that all this obedience to God can never be in vain, nor to our loss; and it tells us that we must all die, and that fleshly pleasures and this transitory world will quickly leave us. There is no more cause to doubt of all or any of this, than whether man he man. Be true to this much, and it will be a great help to all the rest.

II. And as to God's supernatural revelation, hold to God's word, the sacred Bible, written by the special inspiration of the Holy Ghost, as the sufficient records of it.

It is not divine faith if it rest not on divine revelation, nor is it divine obedience which is not given to divine government or command. Man's word is to be believed but as it deserveth, with a human faith, and man's law must be obeyed according to the measure of his authority, with a human obedience; but these are far different from a divine. There is no universal ruler of all the world or church but God; no man is capable of it, nor any council of men. God's law is only in nature, and in the Holy Scripture; and that being the law by which he will judge us, it is the law which is the only divine rule of our faith or judgment, our hearts and lives.

Though all in the Scripture is not of equal clearness or necessity, but a man may be saved that understandeth not a thousand sentences therein, yet all that is necessary to salvation is plainly there contained, and God's law is perfect to its designed use, and needeth no supplement of man's. Hold close to Scripture sufficiency, or you will never know what to hold to. Councils and canons are far more uncertain, and there is no agreement among their subjects which of them are obligatory, and which not, nor any possible way to come to an agreement.

III. Yet use with thankfulness the help of men, for the understanding and obeying the word of God.

Though lawyers, as such, have none of the legislative power, you need their help to understand the use of the law aright. And though no men have power to make laws for the church universal, yet men must be our teachers to understand and use the laws of God. We are not born with faith or knowledge; we know nothing but what is taught us, except what sense or intuition perceiveth, or reason gathereth from thence.

If you ask, Who must we learn of? I answer, of those that know, and have learned themselves. No name, or title, or relation, or habit, will enable any man to teach you that which he knoweth not himself.

1. Children must learn of their parents and tutors.

2. People must learn of their able, faithful pastors and catechisers.

3. All Christians must be teachers by charitable helps to one another.

But teaching and law-making are two things. To teach another is but to show him that same scientific evidence of truth, by which the teacher knoweth it himself, that the learner may know it as he doth. To say, You shall believe that is true which I say is true, and that this is the meaning of it, is not teaching, but law-giving; and to believe such a one, is not to learn or know, though some human belief of our teachers is necessary to learners.

IV. Take nothing as necessary to the being of Christianity and to salvation, which is not recorded in the Scripture, and hath not been held necessary by all true Christians in every age and place.

Not that we must know men first to be true Christians, that by them we may know what Christian truth is, but the plain Scripture tells all men what Christianity is, and by that we know whom to take for Christians. But if anything be new, and risen since the apostles' writing of the Scripture, that can be no point essential to Christianity, else Christianity must be a mutable thing, and not the same now as it was heretofore, or else there were no Christians before this novelty in the world. The church were not the church, nor were any man a Christian, if they lacked any essential part of faith or practice.

But here take heed of sophisters' deceit; though nothing is necessary to salvation but all sound Christians have still believed, yet all is not necessary, or true, or good, which all good Christians have believed or done; much less all which the tempted worse part have held: for though the essence of Christianity has been ever and everywhere the same, yet the opinions of Christians, and their mistakes and faults, have been none of their imitable faith or practice.

Human nature is essentially the same in Adam, and in all men, but the diseases of nature are another thing. If all men have sin and error, so have all churches; their Christianity is of God, but the corruptions and maladies of Christians are not. You must hold nothing but what Christians of old have held as received from God's word; but because they have all some faults and errors, you must not hold and do all those.

V. Maintain the unity of the Spirit in the bond of peace with all true Christians as such, and live in love in the communion of saints.

That is, with them that live in the belief, and in holy obedience to the Christian faith and law. By their fruits you shall know them. The societies of malignants, who suppress true practical knowledge and piety, and hate the best men, and cherish wickedness, and bloodily persecute those that in conscience obey not their usurpations and inventions, are not the communion of saints; wolves, thorns, and thistles, are not the sheep or vines of Christ.

VI. Prefer not any odd or singular sect before the universal consent of the faithful in your learning or communion, so far as the judgment of men is to be regarded.

Though we take not our faith from the number of believers, and though the most be usually none of the best, and some few are much wiser than the most, and in a controversy a few men of such knowledge are to be believed before the multitude of less knowledge, yet Christ is the head of all true Christians, and not of an odd sect or party only; and he hath commanded them all to live as brethren, in love and holy communion; and in all sciences, the greater number of agreeing men are liker to be in the right, than some straggling persons, who show otherwise no more ability than they: at least, which side soever you like best in less necessary points, you must always be in unity with all true Christians, and not unnecessarily differ from them.

VII. Never set a doubtful opinion against a certain truth or duty; reduce not things certain to things uncertain; but contrarily, uncertain things to certain: for instance, it is certain that you ought to live in love and peace with all that are true Christians, and to do good to all, and wrong to none; let not any doubtful difference make you violate this rule, and hate, and slander, and backbite, and hurt them for a doubtful, indifferent, or unnecessary thing; set not our mint or cummin, tithes or ceremonies, against love and justice, and the great and certain things of the law; it is an ill sect or opinion that is against the nature and common duty of Christianity and humanity.

VIII. Faithfully serve Christ as far as you have attained, and be true to all the truth that you know; sin not by omission or practice against the knowledge which you have, lest God in justice give up your understanding to believe a lie.

IX. Remember that all men on earth are ignorant, and know but as in a glass, and in part, and therefore the best have many errors; no man knoweth the smallest grass or worm with an adequate perfect knowledge. And if God bear with multitudes of errors in us all, we must bear with such as are tolerable in each other; it is well if men be humble, and teachable, and willing to know. As we have seen few more imperfect than the sects that have asserted sinless perfection, so we see few so fallible and erroneous as the Roman sect, which pleadeth their infallibility: when they tell you that you must believe their popes and councils, that you may come to an end of controversy, ask them whether we may here hope for any end of ignorance, error, and sin; if not, what hope of ending all controversies before we come to heaven, where ignorance is ended? The controversies against the essentials of Christianity were ended with us all when we became true and adult Christians, and the rest will be lessened as we grow in knowledge. Divinity is not less mysterious than law and science, etc. where controversies abound.

X. Yet stint not yourselves in knowledge, nor say, We have learned enough, but continue as Christ's scholars in learning more and more to the death: the wisest know little and may still increase. There is a great difference in excellency, usefulness, and comfort, between men of clear, digested knowledge, and confused, undigested apprehensions.

These ten rules practiced, will save you from being perplexed with doubts and controversies of all pretenders in religion.

9

Truths to Apply to the Heart

B UT IF YOUR TROUBLE be not about doctrinal controversies, but about your sins, or poverty of grace, and spiritual state, digest well these following truths and counsels, and it will cure you.

I. God's goodness is equal to his greatness; even to that power that ruleth heaven and earth. His attributes are commensurate; and goodness will do good to capable receivers. He loved us when we were enemies; and he is, essentially, love itself.

II. Christ hath freely taken human nature, and made satisfaction for the sins of the world, as full as answereth his ends, and so full that none shall perish for lack of sufficiency in his sacrifice and merits.

III. Upon these merits Christ hath made a law, or covenant of grace, forgiving all sin, and giving freely everlasting life to all that will believingly accept it; so that all men's sins are conditionally pardoned by the tenor of this covenant.

IV. The condition of pardon and life is not that we sin no more, or that by any price we purchase it of God, or by our own works do benefit him, or buy his grace; but only that we believe him, and willingly accept of the mercy which he freely giveth us, according to the nature of the gift; that is, that we accept of Christ as Christ, to justify, sanctify, rule, and save us.

V. God hath commissioned his ministers to proclaim and offer this covenant and grace to all, and earnestly entreat them in his name to accept it, and be reconciled to him; he hath excepted none.

VI. No man that hath this offer is damned, but only those that obstinately refuse it to the last breath.

VII. The day of grace is never so passed to any sinner but still he may have Christ and pardon if he will; and if he have it not, it is because he will not. And the day of grace is so far from being passed, that it is savingly come to all that are so willing; and grace is still offered urgently to all.

VIII. The will is the man in God's account, and what a man truly would be and have, he is, and shall have: consent to the covenant is true grace and conversion, and such have right to Christ and life.

IX. The number and greatness of former sins is no exception against the pardon of any penitent, converted sinner: God pardoneth great and small to such; where sin aboundeth, grace super-aboundeth; and much is forgiven, that men may be thankful, and love much.

X. Repentance is true, though tears and passionate sorrow be defective, when a man had rather leave his sin than keep it, and sincerely, though imperfectly, endeavoureth fully to overcome it; no sin shall damn a man which he more hateth than loveth, and had truly rather leave than keep, and showeth this by true endeavour.

XI. The best man hath much evil, and the worst have some good; but it is that which is preferred, and predominant in the will, which differenceth the godly and the wicked. He that in estimation, choice, and life preferreth God, and heaven, and holiness, before the world, and the pleasure of sin, is a true, godly man, and shall be saved.

XII. The best have daily need of pardon, even for the faultiness of their holiest duties, and must daily live on Christ for pardon.

XIII. Even sins against knowledge and conscience are too oft committed by regenerate men; for they know more than others do, and their consciences are more active: happy were they indeed if they could be as good as they know they should be, and love God as much as they know they should love him, and were clear from all the relicts of passion and unbelief, which conscience tells them are their sins.

XIV. God will not take Satan's temptations to be our sins, but only our not resisting them. Christ himself was tempted to the most heinous sin, even to fall down to the devil and worship him. God will charge Satan's blasphemous temptations on himself alone.

XV. The thoughts, and fears, and troubles, which melancholy, and natural weakness and distemper irresistibly cause, hath much more of bodily disease than of sin, and, therefore, is of the least of sins; and, indeed, no more sin than to burn or be thirsty in a fever, further than as some sin did cause the disease that causeth it, or further than there is left some power in reason to resist them.

XVI. Certainty of our faith and sincerity is not necessary to salvation, but the sincerity of faith itself is necessary. He shall be saved that giveth up himself to Christ, though he know not that he is sincere in doing it. Christ knoweth his own grace, when they that have it know not that it is sound. It is but few true Christians that attain to certainty of salvation; for weak grace clogged with much corruption is hardly known, and usually joined with fear and doubting.

XVII. Probability of sincerity and trust in Christ may cause a man, justly, to live and die in peace and comfort, without proper certainty; else few Christians should live and die in peace; and yet we see by experience that many do so. The common opinion of most church Writers for four hundred years after Christ, was, that the uncontinued sort of Christians might fall from a state of grace, in which, had they continued, they had been saved, and, therefore, that none but strong, confirmed Christians, at most, could be certain of salvation; and many Protestant churches still are of that mind, and yet they live not in despair or terror. No man is certain that he shall not fall as heinously as David and Peter did; and yet while they have no cause to think it likely, they need not live in terror for the uncertainty. No wife or child is certain that the husband or father will not murder them, and yet they may live comfortably, and not fear it.

XVIII. Though faith be so weak, as to be assaulted with doubts whether the gospel be true, and there be any life to come; and though our trust in Christ be not strong enough to banish our fears and troubles; yet if we see so much evidence of credibility in the gospel, and probability of a better life hereafter, as causeth us here to fix our hopes and choice, and to resolve for those hopes to seek first the kingdom of God and his righteousness, and let go all the world rather than sell those hopes, and live a holy life to obtain it, this faith will save us.

XIX. But God's love and promise through Christ so sure a ground for faith and comfort, that it is the great duty and interest of all men, confidently and quietly, to trust him, and then to live in the joy of holy trust and hope.

XX. If any man doubt of his salvation because of the greatness of his sins, the way to quietness is presently to be willing to forsake them. Either he that complaineth is willing to be holy and forsake his sins, or not. If you be not willing to leave them, but love them, and would keep them, why do you complain of them, and mourn for that which you so much love? If your child should cry and roar because his apple is sour, and yet will not be persuaded to forbear to eat it, you would not pity him, but whip him, as perverse. But if you are truly willing to leave it, you are already saved from its damning guilt.

XXI. If you are in doubt of the sincerity of your faith, and other graces, and all your examination leaveth you uncertain, the way is presently to end your doubt by actual giving up yourself to Christ. Do you not know whether you have been hitherto a true believer? You may know that Christ is now offered to you; consent but to the covenant, and accept the offer, and you may be sure that he is yours.

XXII. Bare examining is not always to be done for assurance, but labour to excite and exercise much the grace that you would be assured of; the way to be sure that you believe and love God, is to study the promises and goodness of God, till active faith assure you that you believe, and you love God and glory, till you are assured that you love them.

XXIII. It is not by some extraordinary act, good or bad, that we may be sure what state the soul is in, but by the predominant bent, and drift, and tenor of heart and life.

XXIV. Though we cry out that we cannot believe, and we cannot love God, and we cannot pray aright, Christ can help us; without his grace we can do nothing; but his grace is sufficient for us, and he denieth not his further help when once he hath but made us willing, but hath bid us ask and have; and if any lack wisdom let him ask it of God, who giveth to all liberally, and upbraideth not with former folly, but gives his Spirit to them that ask him.

XXV. This sin, called the blasphemy of the Holy Ghost, is the sin of no one that believeth Jesus to be the Christ, nor of any that fear it, no, nor of every infidel, but only of some few obstinate, unbelieving enemies, for it is only this: when men see such miracles of Christ and his Spirit as should or could convince them that he is of God, and when they have no other shift, they will rather maintain that he is a conjurer, and wrought them by the devil.

XXVI. Though sinful fear is very troublesome, and not to be cherished, God often permitteth and useth it to good, to keep us from being bold with sin, and from those sinful pleasures and love of the world, and presumption, and security, which are far more dangerous, and to take down pride, and keep us in a sensible, watchful state; for just fear is made to preserve us from the hurt and danger feared.

XXVII. He that goeth fearing and trembling to heaven, will there quickly be past all fear, and doubts, and heaviness, forever.

XXVIII. When Christ for our sins was in his agony, and when he cried out, "My God, my God, why hast thou forsaken me?" he was then nevertheless beloved of his Father; and he was tempted that he might succour them that are tempted, and suffered such derision that he might be a compassionate High Priest to sufferers.

XXIX. By how much the more the troubles, and blasphemous temptations, and doubts, and fears of a man are grievous, displeasing, and hateful to him, by so much the more he may be assured that they shall not condemn him, because they are not beloved sins.

XXX. All our troubles are overruled by God; and it is far better for us to be at his choice and disposal than our own, or our dearest friend's; and he hath promised that all things shall work together for our good (Rom. 8:28).

XXXI. A delight in God and goodness, and a joyful, praising frame of soul, from the belief of the love of God through Christ, is far more to be desired than grief and tears, which do but sweep away some dirt, that love, joy, and thankfulness may enter, which are the true evangelical, Christian temper, and likest to the heavenly state.

Digest these truths, and they will cure you.

10

Helps for Those Who are Depressed

BUT IF MELANCHOLY HAVE got head already, there must be, besides what is said, some other and proper remedies used; and the difficulty is great, because the disease makes them self-conceited, unreasonable, willful, and unruly, and they will hardly be persuaded that the disease is in their bodies, but only in the souls, and will not believe but they have reason for all what they think and do; or if they confess the contrary, they plead disability, and say, We can think and do no otherwise than we do.

• But supposing that there is some use of reason left, I will give them yet some further counsel; and what they cannot do, their friends must help them to their power, which I shall add.

1. Consider that it should be easy for you in your confounding, troubling thoughts, to perceive that your

understandings are not now so sound and strong as other men's; and therefore be not willful and self-conceited, and think not that your thoughts are righter than theirs, but believe wiser men, and be ruled by them.

Answer me this question: Do you know any minister, or friend, that is wiser than yourself? If you say no, how foolishly proud are you? If you say yea, then ask the minister, or friend, what he thinketh of your condition, and believe him, and be ruled by him rather than by your infirm self.

2. Do you find that your troubles do you more good or hurt? Do they make you fitter or unfitter to believe and love God, and rejoice in him and praise him? If you feel that they are against all that is good, you may be sure that they are so far from the devil's temptations, and are pleasing to him; and will you cherish or plead for the work of Satan, which you find is against yourselves and God?

3. Avoid your musings, and exercise not your thoughts now too deeply, nor too much. Long meditation is a duty to some, but not to you, no more than it is a man's duty to go to church that hath his leg broken, or his foot out of joint: he must rest and ease it till it be set again, and strengthened. You may live in the faith and fear of God, without setting yourself to deep, disturbing thoughts.

Those that will not obey this counsel, their friends must rouse them from their musings, and call them off to something else.

4. Therefore you must not be much alone, but always in some pleasing, cheerful company: solitariness doth but cherish musings.

Nor must such be long in secret prayer, but more in public prayer with others.

5. Let those thoughts which you have be laid out on the most excellent things: pore not all on yourselves, and on your distempered hearts; the best may find there much matter of trouble. As millstones wear themselves if they go when they have no corn, so do the thoughts of such as think not of better things than their own hearts. If you have any power of your own thoughts, force them to think most of these four things:

1. The infinite goodness of God, who is fuller of love than the sun is of light.

2. Of the unmeasurable love of Christ in man's redemption, and of the sufficiency of his sacrifice and merits.

3. Of the free covenant and offer of grace, which giveth pardon and life to all that do not prefer the pleasure of sin before it, and obstinately refuse it to the last.

4. Of the unconceivable glory and joy which all the blessed have with Christ, and which God hath promised with his oath and seal, to all that consent to the covenant of grace, and are willing to be saved and ruled by Christ. These thoughts will cure melancholy fears.

5. Do not yourselves often to a complaining talk, but talk most of the great mercies of God which you have received. Dare you deny them? If not, are they not worthier of your discourse than your present sufferings? Let not all men know that you are in your troubles: complaining doth but feed them, and it discourageth them to none but your secret counselors and friends. Use much to speak of the love of God, and the riches of grace, and it will divert and sweeten your sourer thoughts.

6. Especially, when you pray, resolve to spend most of your time in thanksgiving and praising God. If you cannot do it with the joy that you should, yet do it as you can. You have not the power of your comforts; but have you no power of your tongues? Say not that you are unfit for thanks and praises, unless you had a praising heart, and were the children of God; for every man, good and bad, is bound to praise God, and to be thankful for all that he hath received, and to do it as well as he can, rather than leave it undone: and most Christians are without assurance of their adoption; and must they, therefore, forbear all praise and thanksgiving to God? Doing it as

you can is the way to be able to do it better. Thanksgiving stirreth up thankfulness in the heart, but by your objection you may perceive what the devil driveth at, and gets by your melancholy. He would turn you off from all thankfulness to God, and from the very mention of his love and goodness in your praises.

7. When vexatious or blasphemous thoughts are thrust into your mind by Satan, neither give them entertainment, nor yet be excessive troubled at them: first, use that reason and power that is left you resolutely to cast them out, and turn your thoughts to somewhat else; do not say, I cannot. If you can no otherwise command and turn away your thoughts, rise up and go into some company or to some employment which will divert you, and take them up. Tell me what you would do if you heard a grumbling woman in the street reviling you, or heard an atheist there talk against God? Would you stand still to hear them, or would you talk it out again with them, or rather go from them, and disdain to hear them, or debate the case with such as they? Do you, in your case, when Satan casts in ugly, or despairing, or murmuring thoughts, go away from them to some other thoughts or business.

If you cannot do this of yourself, tell your friend when the temptation cometh; and it is his duty who hath the care of you to divert you with some other talk or words, or force you into diverting company.

Yet be not too much troubled at the temptation, for trouble of mind doth keep the evil matter in your memory, and so increase it, as pain of a sore draws the blood and spirits to the place. And this is the design of Satan, to give you troubling thoughts, and then to cause more by being troubled at those; and so, for one thought, and trouble to cause another, and that another, and so on, as waves in the sea do follow each other. To be tempted is common to the best. I told you to what idolatry Christ was tempted. When you feel such thoughts, thank God, that Satan cannot force you to love them, or consent.

8. Again, still remember what a comfortable evidence you carry about with you that your sin is not damning, while you feel that you love it not, but hate it, and are weary of it. Scarce any sort of sinners have so little pleasure in their sins as the melancholy, nor so little desire to keep them; and only beloved sins undo men.

Be sure that you live not idly, but in some constant business of a lawful calling, so far as you have bodily strength. Idleness is a constant sin, and labour is a duty. Idleness is but the devil's home for temptation, and for unprofitable, distracting musings. Labour profiteth others, and ourselves: both soul and body need it. Six days must you labour, and must not eat the bread of idleness (Prov. 31). God hath made it our duty, and will bless us in his appointed way.

I have known grievous, despairing melancholy cured, and turned into a life of godly cheerfulness, principally by setting upon constancy and diligence in the business of families and callings. It turns the thoughts from temptations, and leaveth the devil no opportunity: it pleaseth God if done in obedience, and it purifieth the distempered blood. Though thousands of poor people that live in penury, and have wives and children that must also feel it, one would think should be distracted with griefs and cares, yet few of them fall into the disease of melancholy, because labour keepeth the body sound, and leaveth them no leisure for melancholy musings: whereas, in London, and great towns, abundance of women that never sweat with bodily work, but live in idleness, especially when from fullness they fall into poverty, are miserable objects, continually vexed, and near distraction with discontent and a restless mind.

If you will not be persuaded to business, your friends, if they can, should force you to it.

And if the devil turn religious as an angel of light, and tell you that this is but turning away your thoughts from God, and that worldly thoughts and business are unholy, and fit for worldly men; tell him that Adam was in innocency to dress and keep his garden, and Noah that had all the world was to be husbandman, and Abraham, Isaac, and Jacob kept sheep and cattle, and Paul was a tent-maker, and Christ himself is justly supposed to have worked at his supposed father's trade, as he went on fishing with his disciples. And Paul saith, idleness is disorderly walking, and he that will not work let him not eat. God made soul and body, and hath commanded work to both.

And if Satan would drive you unseasonably upon longer secret prayer than you can bear, remember that even sickness will excuse the sick from that sort of duty which they are unable for, and so will your disease; and the unutterable groans of the spirit are accepted.

If you have privacy out of hearing, I would give you this advice, that instead of long meditation, or long secret prayer, you will sing a psalm of praise to God, such as the twenty-third, or the one hundred and thirty-third, &c. This will excite your spirit to that sort of holy affection which is much more acceptable to God, and suitable to the hopes of a believer, than your repining troubles are.

11

Duties Toward Depressed Persons

B UT YET I HAVE NOT done with the duty of those that take care of distressed, melancholy persons, especially husbands to their wives (for it is much more frequently the disease of women than of men), when the disease disableth them to help themselves, the most of their helps, under God, must be from others; and this is of two sorts: 1. In prudent carriage to them; 2. In medicine and diet; a little of both.

1. A great part of their cure lieth in pleasing them, and avoiding all displeasing things, as far as lawfully can be done. Displeasedness is much of the disease; and a husband that hath such a wife is obliged to do his best to cure her, both in charity, and by his relative bond, and for his own peace. It is a great weakness in some men, that if they have wives, who by natural passionate weakness, or by melancholy or infirmity, are willful and will not

yield to reason, they show their anger at them to their further provocation. You took her in marriage for better and for worse, for sickness and health. If you have chosen one that, as a child, must have everything that she crieth for, and must be spoken fair, and as it was rocked in the cradle, or else it will be worse, you must condescend to do it, and so bear the burden which you have chosen, as may not make it heavier to you. Your passion and sourness towards a person that cannot cure her own unpleasing carriage, is a more inexcusable fault and folly than hers, who hath not the power of reason as you have.

If you know any lawful thing that will please them in speech, in company, in apparel, in rooms, in attendance, give it them: if you know at what they are displeased, remove it. I speak not of the distracted, that must be mastered by force, but of the sad and melancholy: could you devise how to put them in a pleased condition you might cure them.

2. As much as you can, divert them from the thoughts which are their trouble; keep them on some other talks and business; break in upon them, and interrupt their musings; rouse them out of it, but with loving importunity; suffer them not to be long alone; get fit company to them, or them to it; especially, suffer them not to be idle, but drive or draw them to some pleasing works which may stir the body, and employ the thoughts.

If they are addicted to reading, let it not be too long, nor any books that are unfit for them; and rather let another read to them than themselves. Dr. Sibbes's books, and some useful, pleasing history or chronicles, or news of great matters abroad in the world, may do somewhat to divert them.

3. Often set before them the great truths of the gospel which are fittest to comfort them; and read them informing, comforting books; and live in a loving, cheerful manner with them.

4. Choose for them a skillful, prudent minister of Christ, both for their secret counsel and public audience; one that is skilled in such cases, and one that is peaceable, and not contentious, erroneous, or fond of odd opinions; one that is rather judicious in his preaching and praying than passionate, except when he urgeth the gospel doctrines of consolation, and then the more fervently the better; and one that they much esteem and reverence, and will regardfully hear.

5. Labour to convince them frequently how great a wrong it is to the God of infinite love and mercy, and to a Saviour who hath so wonderfully expressed his love, to think hardlier of him than they would do of a friend, yea, or of a moderate enemy; and so hardly to be persuaded of that love which hath been manifested by the most stupendous miracle. Had they but a father, husband, or

friend, that had ventured his life for them, and given them all that ever they had, were it not a shameful ingratitude and injury to suspect still that they intended all against them, and designed mischief to them, and did not love them? How hath God and our Saviour deserved this? And many that say it is not God that they suspect, but themselves, do but hide their misery this mistake, while they deny God's greatest mercies; and though they would fain have Christ and grace, will not believe that God who offereth it them will give it them, but think he is one that will remedilessly damn a poor soul that desireth to please him, and had rather have his grace than all the sinful pleasures of the world.

6. Carry them oft abroad into strange company. Usually they reverence strangers, and strange faces do divert them, especially traveling into other parts, if they can hear the motion.

7. It is a useful way, if you can, to engage them in comforting others that are deeper in distresses than they; for this will tell them that their case is not singular, and they will speak to themselves while they speak to others. One of the chief means which cured my fears of my soul's condition, about forty-eight years ago, was oft comforting others that had the same doubts, whose lives persuaded me of their sincerity.

And it would be a pretty diversion to send to them some person that is in some error, which they are most against, to dispute it with them, that, while they whet their wits to convince them, and confute them, it may turn their thoughts from their own distress. Forester tells us that a melancholy patient of his, who was a papist, was cured when the Reformation came into the country, by eager and oft disputing against it. A better cause may better do it.

12

Medical Care for the Depressed

I F OTHER MEANS WILL not do, neglect not medicine; and though they will be averse to it, as believing that the disease is only in the mind, they must be persuaded or forced to it. I have known the lady deep in melancholy, who a long time would neither speak, nor take medicine, nor endure her husband to go out of the room, and with the restraint and grief he died, and she was cured by drugs put down her throat with a pipe by force.

If it were, as some of them fancy, a possession of the devil, it is possible physic might cast him out, for if you cure the melancholy, his bed is taken away, and the advantage gone by which he worketh. Cure the choler, and the choleric operations of the devil cease. It is by means and humours in us that he worketh.

But choose a physician who is specially skilled in this disease, and hath cured many others. Meddle not with women, and ignorant boasters, nor with young, unexperienced men, nor with hasty, busy, over-doing, venturous men, who cannot have time to study the patient's temper and disease, but choose experienced, cautious men.

Medicinal remedies and theological are not often to be given together by the same hand; but in this case of perfect complication of the maladies of mind and body, I think it not unfit, if I do it not unskillfully. My advice is, that they that can have an ancient, skillful, experienced, honest, careful, circumspect physician, neglect not to use him.

The disease called *melancholy* is formally in the spirits, whose distemper unfits them for their office, in serving the imagination, understanding, memory, and affections; so, by their distemper, the thinking faculty is diseased and become like an inflamed eye, or a foot that is sprained or out of joint, disabled for its proper work.

The matter which is the root and foundation is usually a depravation of the mass of blood, which is the vehicle of the spirits; and that is usually accompanied with some diseases of the stomach, spleen, liver, or other parts, which are for the due concoction, motion, and purification of the blood; which diseases are so various, that they are seldom the same in many persons, and hardly known to the wisest physicians. The spleen is most commonly accused, and often guilty, and the stomach, pancreas, mesentery, omentum, liver, yea, and reins, not rarely are the root, sometimes by obstructing humours, and that of several qualities, and sometimes by stones, and sometimes by various sorts of humours, and sometimes by vesicles; but obstructed, if not tumefied, spleens, are most suspected.

Such a black, distinct humour called melancholy, which hath oft of old been accused, is rarely, if ever, found in any, unless you will call either blood or excrementitious humours by that name, which are grown black by mortification, for lack of motion and spirits. But the blood itself may be called melancholy blood, when it hath contracted that distemper and pravity by feculency, sluggishness, or adustion, melancholy effects.

But sometimes persons that are sound, are suddenly cast into melancholy by a fright, or by the death of a friend, or by some great loss or cross, or some sad tidings, even in an hour, which shows that it cometh not always from any humour called melancholy, nor for any foregoing disease at all.

But the very act of the mind doth suddenly disorder the passions, and perturb the spirits; and the disturbed spirits, in time, vitiate the blood which containeth them; and the vitiated blood doth, in time, vitiate the viscera and parts which it passeth through; and so the disease beginning in the senses and soul, doth draw first the spirits, and then the humours, and then the parts, into the fellowship, and soul and body are sick together.

And it is of great use to the physician to know where the depravation did begin, whether in the mind or in the body; and if in the body, whether in the blood, or in the viscera, for the cure must be fitted accordingly.

And yet the melancholy brains may be eased, and the mental depravation much kept under, though an obstructed, yea, a scarified spleen, continue uncured many years.

And though the disease begin in the mind and spirits, and the body be yet sound, yet physic, even purging, often cureth it, though the patient say that drugs cannot cure souls, for the soul and body are wonderfully co-partners in their diseases and cure; and if we know not how it doth it, yet when experience telleth us that it doth it, we have reason to use such means.

The devil hath another cure for the sad and melancholy than such as I have here prescribed, which is to cast away all belief of the immortality of the soul and the life to come, or at least not to think of it; and for to take religion to be a superstitious, needless fancy; and for to laugh at the threatenings of the Scripture, and to go to play-houses, and cards, and dice, and to drink and play away melancholy: honest recreations are very good for melancholy persons, if we could get them to use them; but, alas! This satanical cure is but like the witches' bargain with the devil, who promiseth them much, but payeth them with shame and utter misery. The end of that mirth is uncurable sorrow, if timely repentance cure not the cause.

The garrison of Satan in the hearts of sinners is strongly kept when they are in peace, but when they have fooled away time, and mercy, and hope, die they must, there is no remedy; and to go merrily and unbelievingly to hell, after all God's calls and warnings, will be no abatement of their torment; to go out of the world in the guilt of sin, and to end life before they would know the use of it, and to undergo God's justice for the mad contempt of Christ and grace, will put a sad end to all their mirth, for, "There is no peace to the wicked, saith my God" (Isa. 48:22; 57:21).

But Christ saith to his mourners, "Blessed are you that mourn, for you shall be comforted" (Matt. 5:4); and, "Ye shall weep and lament, but the world shall rejoice; and ye shall be sorrowful, but your sorrow shall be turned into joy" (John 16:20). And Solomon knew that the house of mourning was better than the house of feasting; and that the heart of the wise is in the house of mourning, but the heart of fools is in the house of mirth (Eccl. 7:2-4); but holy joy of faith and hope is best of all.

For additional titles from Ichthus Publications, log on to:

www.ichthuspublications.com.

Printed in Great Britain
by Amazon

85598905R00056